We're Falling
Through Space

Published by 404 Ink Limited
www.404Ink.com
@404Ink

Editing: Laura Jones & Heather McDaid
Typesetting: Laura Jones
Cover design: Luke Bird
Co-founders and publishers of 404 Ink:
Heather McDaid & Laura Jones

Print ISBN: 978-1-912489-76-3
Ebook ISBN: 978-1-912489-77-0

Printed and bound in Great Britain by Clays Ltd, Elcograf S.p.A.

We're Falling Through Space

Doctor Who and Celebrating the Mundane

J. David Reed

Inklings

Contents

Pronouns Usage

When referring to a male-presenting Doctor, he/him pronouns are used.

When referring to a female-presenting Doctor, she/her pronouns are used.

When referring to the Doctor in a wider sense, they/them pronouns are used.

Spoilers

Please note there are multiple spoilers throughout *We're Falling Through Space* for the entirety of the *Doctor Who* franchise. Specific episodes that are discussed in order of appearance:

Chapter 3: Dimensions

Interlude 2: in

Chapter 4: Space

Conclusion: The Future

Introduction
The Past

'You can fill your life with work and food and sleep,
or you could go... anywhere.'
– The Ninth Doctor.
Episode 1, Series 1
(Rose)

It's March 26th, 2005, and I am nine years old. The house is buzzing with the hubbub of an almost-party. We're hosting family friends from down south, but things have started to calm down after a day of catching up, snacking and, for the adults, drinking. Outside, it's getting darker, and we're full of picky bits from dinner as we settle down in front of the foot-deep CRT TV for a night of the BBC's best.

I don't remember if we'd planned to watch it, if I was excited, or if I even knew what it was. I have since learned that my parents had, at best, a passing knowledge of *Doctor Who* from their own childhoods. They knew of the time-and-space travelling man known as 'the Doctor', that there was a spaceship called the TARDIS that looked like a '60s police box, that the Doctor was an alien of the 'Time Lord' species, and that his greatest enemy was the Daleks. They definitely knew that it was camp sci-fi fun for the whole family.

They also knew it was something my down-south friends and I would enjoy being distracted by while they continued the day-drinking into evening. Little did they know I was being introduced to a passionate obsession that would carry me through my life for decades.

As the BBC logo faded away, we saw our first images. First, the vast edges of our solar system, space, and a promise of where we were going. Panning across blurry lands, we're bearing down on planet Earth, zooming in on the UK, London, a block of flats. We're in the bedroom of Rose Tyler, an average nineteen-year-old human, awaking groggily to an alarm. We've swooped in from the depths space to land somewhere familiar – a morning before work.

I didn't realise it at the time but these first few shots that focus on a recognisable human as opposed to our eponymous hero, this revival of *Doctor Who* (known as

Nu Who) articulated a philosophy to me: *No matter how enormous the universe may be, we care about the beings who exist here.* It's as though the show itself was saying, *Yes, yes there is space and sci-fi to explore, of course, but* first, *let's pay attention to how this nineteen-year-old wakes up every morning. That's far more interesting.*

Growing up with *Doctor Who,* I feel I know the show quite intimately though my own experience will not be the same as a fellow fan, nor a more casual viewer. Either way, so we're all on the same page before diving into my interpretations of the show's celebration of the mundane, let's cover some of the basics of *Doctor Who* history.

Originally broadcast in November 1963, *Doctor Who* is a British sci-fi adventure following the adventures of 'the Doctor' and his rotating cast of companions who join him on perilous adventures across time and space. The Doctor is a Time Lord, an alien from a planet named Gallifrey. When the time comes, instead of dying, a Time Lord is able to regenerate, meaning their physical appearance, age, and personality changes. In terms of the show's production, this means a change of actor from series to series.

In his trusty time-hopping ship, the TARDIS (an acronym for Time and Relative Dimensions in Space) the Doctor and his companions journey in both the past and present with outcomes both educational and fantastical.

They encounter famous villains like the Daleks and the Cybermen, as well as fellow Time Lord, the Master.

The original *Doctor Who* ran from 1963 to 1989 before it was cancelled by the then-new Head of Series at the BBC. An attempted relaunch in 1996 consisted of a half-American produced film starring Paul McGann as the Eighth Doctor failed to produce anything further. The current era, *NuWho*, relaunched in 2005 with Christopher Eccleston as the Ninth Doctor, is where I'll be focusing, through the subsequent Doctors and their stories that have bolstered the show's international presence to previously unprecedented levels.

Like most good quality sci-fi, *Doctor Who*'s appeal exists in its ability to go anywhere, tell stories about anything to an almost infinitesimal degree. From ancient Rome to the end of the universe, *Doctor Who* has done it, though these spectacles are often mirrored with a crucial focus on the human every day, the mundane lives of mundane people from all over the world are so often the beating heart of the show. Like any TV show that has existed over decades, it must adapt to its evolving audience to stay fresh and reflective of the world it's in. *Doctor Who*'s original creators and writers figured this out early in its tenure and has been able to survive, more or less, from the '60s to the 2020s. The secret? Regeneration. Despite the masses of alternative entertainment and decades of history, re-inventing itself every few years offers regular jumping-on points for new fans and for new staff on the show. It mutates, changes the roster of characters without issue, revamps classic monster designs, explores new adventures in new places, hires fresh talent behind the camera.

In 2010, along with the departure of David Tennant's Tenth Doctor, Russell T. Davies stepped down as show-runner, replaced by Steven Moffat, who then departed years later with the regeneration of Peter Capaldi's Twelfth Doctor into Jodie Whittaker's Thirteenth, when the role transferred to Chris Chibnal, who leaves alongside Whittaker as the series approached the 60th anniversary, ready for the next era. Every regeneration, in front of and behind the camera, invites fans to discover 'their' Doctor, to fall in love with the show anew.

Audiences don't just understand this cycle, most look forward to it. *Doctor Who* takes advantage of its frequent reinvention, with Whittaker's Thirteenth Doctor being the first female, and Ncuti Gatwa's casting as the first Black Doctor – aside from Jo Martin's 'Fugitive Doctor', the first Black woman to play the Time Lord in a version set somewhere in the past, erased from the Doctor's memory. The show grows to reflect the progressive sensibilities expected by the majority of modern audiences, and the diversity of the world, the universe, around us. Of course, there unfortunately exists a vocal minority who mourn the loss of white, male Doctors, even though you'd think twelve in a row was a pretty good run and a progressive, inclusive change would be welcome, but no fandom is perfect and *Doctor Who*'s audience is no exception.

Just as no fandom is perfect, neither are the humans in *Doctor Who*, which is why, time and time again, beneath the global presence and the intergalactic spectacle of the show itself, *Doctor Who* always brings its focus back to the people of Earth and takes joy in looking at the wonder of everyday life in all its beauty and mundanity.

Once you've stepped through those deep-blue TARDIS doors there is no going back, so a couple of disclaimers before we cross the threshold. This isn't a 'history of', or a 'I like *Doctor Who* because…' polemic. In fact, I should probably be honest with you and say that in all truthfulness, despite what this book's subtitle says, *Doctor Who* doesn't really celebrate the mundane *exactly*. As we'll later see, the Doctor operates by the philosophy that every person is extraordinary and far from mundane. The celebration of the mundane is up to us, the viewers, as we sit back and watch the drama unfold, empathising with the trials and tribulations the companions are dragged through as the Doctors push them to their full potential and limits, sometimes at an alarmingly traumatic rate.

We're Falling Through Space is an interaction with what I identify to be the show's most interesting theses through the lens of celebrating the human mundane; the cup of tea or coffee we make in the morning, the friendships we carry and lose in life, the routines we love and hate, the vinegar-soaked chippies we have at night. I hope to show you how *Doctor Who,* from 2005 to the time of writing in 2023, embodies a love for the 'normal', the non-fantastic, the non-sci-fi, and how all these stories paint an exceptionally ordinary picture of humanity.

'We're all stories in the end,' as Matt Smith's Doctor says. 'Just make it a good one, eh?'

Chapter 1
Time

> 'By the way, did I mention it also travels in time?'
> – The Ninth Doctor.
> Episode 1, Series 1
> (Rose)

Whether you're a die-hard fan or not, you probably know that *Doctor Who* is about time travel. Or, at least, it's the crux of the show's momentum, one element that remains constant between the original rendition and *NuWho*. While 'time' is the first letter of the Doctor's acronymically-named TARDIS and travelling across ages is, of course, the driver of the show, *Doctor Who* is not about time travel in the way that *Jaws* is not about beach safety.

Doctor Who's core conceit enables it to explore conversations about our human relationship to time and how, eventually, we all go through changes. By dropping our beloved characters into unusual settings and periods – whether that's the fall of Pompeii, a space station orbiting a black hole, or another universe altogether – time travel asks what it all means on a comparatively lower, more mundane level – the human level. Episode 'The End of the World' gives us our first insight into how Rose Tyler, a bottle-blonde nineteen-year-old from London, would see the titular event, the Doctor having brought her to the literal end of planet Earth.

'Earth-Death in twenty minutes,' chimes an overly polite tannoy as Rose argues with the Doctor about being brought so far away from home without a second thought, joking that she can't exactly 'call a taxi'. With a bit of 'jiggery-pokery', the Doctor alters her phone to make calls across time and Rose's first instinct from billions of years in the future, looking down at a dying Earth, is to call her mum, Jackie Tyler. This isn't about the world ending, not really. It's about calling home when you're scared.

Consider those moments when it feels like the whole world is against you. Like there has been a concerted effort by the universe to make sure you have as little agency as possible, forcing you to confront a situation where there is nothing you can do you change it. From losing a loved one, being lost in a supermarket as a child, to big, consequence-fuelled worries at work and everything in between. No experience is universal, yet I'm willing to bet a vast majority of people know how it feels to be powerless, to varying degrees. But the Doctor has a time machine, they can go anywhere and save the universe over and over again. How can a character like that feel powerless? How can they be manipulated to give up? More importantly, how does the Doctor give up, without grinding the story to a complete halt, without admitting defeat? The answer is embedded within 'fixed points.'

Fixed points in history (events that can't be meddled with, avoided, or outmanoeuvred) are commonly used by *Doctor Who* to analyse existential explanations of who the Doctor's modern companions are, how they work, and why certain occurrences simply have to happen, whether good or bad, that the Doctor can't stop. Three episodes come to mind when thinking about how fixed points unify wider tragedy and the predictability of humanity – empathy.

'Father's Day' presents Rose wishing to see how her father, Pete, died when she was just a child, and for him to not die alone. Instead of being a bystander to this event firmly fixed in the past, a twist of understandable teenage impulsivity causes her to save him. It's a truth universally acknowledged across all time travel fiction that changing the past can have drastic repercussions in the future or present (see *Back to the Future*, *The Butterfly Effect* and so many others) and it's no different here. Rose causes a wound in time that invites vicious Reapers in to 'sterilise the wound', i.e. repair the timeline to the fixed point it should be where Pete Tyler is dead. We see here that fixed points are not *technically* unchangeable – Rose's decision does indeed change the fixed point. It's just incredibly dangerous to anyone involved, if not universe-ending, that's all.

In 'The Wedding of River Song', the Doctor's death by a lake in Utah is established as a fixed point in time when mysterious semi-companion River is supposed to shoot him dead. In this episode, she refuses. She uses up her ammunition shooting the ground and spares the Doctor, confounding another fixed point – something that is supposed to be impossible, if not, again, *incredibly dangerous*. This time, an entire alternate universe is created, because, in the Doctor's words, 'A fixed point has been altered. Time is disintegrating.' It's never explained exactly how this law of time-manipulation is broken here and in 'Father's Day', but the while the rules change either through lofty ambition or plot holes, the message is clear – don't try to change fixed points. A message easy to misinterpret as persuading the episodes' viewers to give up their omnipotent agency. *What happens, happens. Don't try to change it.*

For me, there is a nuanced truth in this flexibility of space-time law. When my grandfather, Brian Reed, passed away in 2008, I was about thirteen years old. My sister was young, too young to go to the funeral, so I stayed with her at a friend's house instead of saying goodbye. A part of me wished for a *long* time that I could take that back, do something differently. Maybe even selfishly leave her alone with the friend so I could attend the funeral. But *Doctor Who* is right, it doesn't matter. What happened, happened. The way forward is to accept reality and not make up hypothetical what-could-have-beens.

In 'The Fires of Pompeii', the fixed point isn't the death of a single person but the death of thousands. Throughout the episode, the Doctor and companion Donna are at each other's throats whether the eruption of Vesuvius *must* happen. Donna, thinking of all the people who are about to die, finds this inevitability abhorrent, but the Doctor is pretty much set in his ways, there's no getting around this event in history – until it transpires that the eruption of Pompeii doesn't occur because of natural phenomena. Instead, the Doctor is the one to push a big button that creates the disaster. 'If Pompeii is destroyed then it's not just history. It's me.' Together, the Doctor and Donna go through with it to maintain the fixed point, hand in hand. They cannot undo what happens here, but they are able to help each other through it, sharing the weight. Shortly afterward,

Donna is shaken by what they have done, pleading with the Doctor to give in, just a little.

'Just someone. Please,' Donna asks of him. She understands that this is a rule he can't break and if he was able to stop it, he would have done it without hesitation. Still, she pleads. 'Just someone.'

Every fixed point highlights the humanity of each companion and subverts the typical standpoint of the companion being subservient to the Doctor's knowledge and intelligence. Time after time, companions see the Doctor shrug in the face of fixed points, and they say 'No.'

I won't let my father die.

I won't let you *die.*

Just save someone.

This emotional mercifulness shines through the characters in ways that are alien to the Doctor, whose impulse is to accept tragedy and walk away. Rose, River and Donna all function as audience stand-ins during these stories, exemplifying empathy and love, highlighting the human desire to care in contrast to the Doctor who relies on logic in these terrible situations, trying to think 'above' the love. It holds up the human instincts of warmth and responsibility to each other as what really matters. In dire circumstances, it is vitally important that we care about each other first. *Doctor Who* knows that, even if the Doctor themselves can be a bit slow to the realisation.

Naturally, there are exceptions to rules, even fixed point narratives. Mere episodes after 'The Fires of Pompeii', the 'Waters of Mars' shows the Mars space station in 2059, Bowie Base One, explode with everybody within it dying. This tragedy inspires other humans to venture out into the stars, kick-starting humanity's space-faring age. Another fixed point. This episode specifically focuses on the commander of Bowie Base One, Adelaide Brooke.

'Imagine it, Adelaide,' the Doctor says. 'If you began a journey that takes the human race all the way out into the stars […] And then your granddaughter, you inspire her.' Adelaide's death is the final piece of the puzzle for history to happen as it's supposed to.

The story goes on. People are morphed into water-zombies and the Doctor, in typical fashion in the face of history's fixed points, walks away, knowing nothing good can come from fighting it. However, he has a change of heart when he hears the voices of those dying around him as he walks back the TARDIS. He hears them via a headset, screaming and fighting, eventually deciding that he has the power to change that, to stop just one person from suffering. He saves Adelaide, taking her back to Earth, setting her down in front of her house. Adelaide knows, after the Doctor's speech, that her death is what inspires her family to lead humanity into the stars and without that tragedy, humanity will stay on earth, never to venture outwards and progress. In one of the darkest moments of modern *Doctor Who*, the Doctor walks triumphantly to the TARDIS while Adelaide walks back into her house. From outside, we see her enter the house and close the door, followed by a flash of light and a bang. An insert flashes up, a biography of Adelaide on a computer screen. Her place of death appears, as it fades from one word to another, 'Mars' to 'Earth'. Nothing else changes. Nothing *can* change. It's challenging, but it's also true of *Doctor Who*'s core values. Where Rose, River, and Donna each wanted to save one person (Rose's father, the Doctor, 'anyone'), Adelaide's actions were in the name of humanity – *she* was the one to maintain the fixed point this time, not the Doctor. Her empathy and willingness to give to ensure the success of those who come after her embodies the generous, caring values *Doctor Who* has already upheld.

Ultimately, *Doctor Who*'s time travel enables its human characters to act on their regrets. On one hand, it's shown as a sort of hubris, that the universe operates on a cold, calculated level which contradicts our minds, full of emotion. But, on the other hand, it speaks to a very common, mundane question. Given the chance, isn't there something *you* would do differently?

Some major character exits in *Doctor Who* illustrate the turmoil of being teased with a better life, only to have it unjustly taken away.

In 'The Eleventh Hour', as a little girl, Amy Pond meets Matt Smith's Doctor before he vanishes and fumbles the return journey, finally meeting her as an adult. Amy, played by Karen Gillan, is dubbed 'the girl who waited'. Despite the whimsy in her first interaction with the Doctor, waiting for him to return significantly impacted her childhood and development, so much so that is hard to present with *quite* the same whimsy.

'Twelve years and four psychiatrists,' she tells him after he realises that she is the little girl he met moments ago – it's over a decade for her. 'They said you weren't real.' Time, and the way the Doctor navigates it compared to how Amy experiences it, caused her life to go down a completely different path, a more mundane one. Until now.

During series six, this particular duo's second series of adventures, the Doctor dies. At least, the event of his death is broadcast as the truth across the universe in 'The Wedding of River Song', leading Amy to believe he's really gone. She and Rory (Amy's best friend turned fiancé turned husband) have moved in together, the house a goodbye gift from the Doctor two episodes earlier, and real life seems to be settling in. The next time we see them, the Ponds haven't seen the Doctor in at least two years and though it's a brief moment on Christmas day lasting only a minute or two of screen time, things seem… *normal.* Amy is in a comfy jumper and wielding

17

a water pistol. It's a jolly, cheerful, and reunion meant to show how life's paths can always diverge again. The Doctor and Amy, reunited!

However, it's revealed that one of their previous traumatic adventures led to Amy becoming infertile, leading to a consistent communication breakdown between her and Rory. The next visit from the Doctor in the subsequent series reveals that the Ponds are getting divorced. Not quite the happy ending we were promised for the couple, but the Doctor is able to reconcile them. The Doctor repeatedly drops in then bounces away, leaving Amy and Rory to constantly deal with the ramifications, only for him to do it again while they try to live a normal life.

In the episode preceding Amy and Rory's series seven exit, 'The Power of Three', there is more attention given to the home lives of the Ponds before we say goodbye forever. Taking place largely in their home on Earth, moments highlight how they are slowly drifting away from the Doctor and his time-and-space-hopping adventures.

'I said yes,' Rory says after being offered a full-time position. 'I committed.'

'And I committed to being a bridesmaid, months in advance,' Amy replies, as they sit in bed, cups of tea comfortably in-hand. 'Like I know I'm going to be here.'

'Did real life just get started?' Rory asks.

'I like it,' Amy says with a frown.

'So do I.' Rory takes a sip of tea. The Ponds seem almost shocked with themselves. There is something about the mundane they find all too charming. A montage of quick-fire snippets of non-episode adventures follows, with Amy and Rory looking either exhausted or annoyed, before cutting to them happy at a party on Earth. The galactic adventures are no longer what they were.

Amy's final adventure lands her and Rory in 1930s New York, permanently, with the Doctor unable to ever visit or save them. At this point, this seems like a mercy for all he's done to their lives. Amy leaves the Doctor a farewell, hidden on the last page of a novel that he knows he will find, letting him know she and Rory lived full lives. It's not until the Doctor is forcibly removed from their lives that Amy and Rory get to enjoy normality. While it may not be in the era they expected, it's a life that will be free of apocalypses, aliens, or the Doctor. Considering how much the Doctor had impacted – and, some might argue, *ruined* – their lives, it's possible to see this as a happy ending for them.

Time is change. Change is a normal, exciting, frustrating, and inevitable part of life. Just as normal, and just as inevitable, *Doctor Who* argues, is the instinct to fight it, to shape it.

Sometimes, like Rose in 'Father's Day', we lose. Rose was faced with a change in her life that she saw as a negative one, and assumed that with her father alive, life would be better. She lost, not because she was *wrong*, but because she was acting out regret in real time, trying to undo what was done. But change in *Doctor Who* is not simply apocalyptic, the Doctor brings with them the universe and offers the normal people he meets the ultimate change of scenery. There is, in a sense, a dichotomy of positive and negative change. Good outcomes are just as likely as bad ones. A balance.

In 'Vincent and the Doctor', the Doctor, Amy and Rory meet Vincent van Gogh. They witness his creativity, his depression, his mania, all with the knowledge that van Gogh himself lacks – knowledge of his impending suicide. Amy, through their intervention, believes that they might have been able to stop it, only to be met with the fact that they didn't change anything. Or, at least, she doesn't think so. The Doctor sees the other side.

'The way I see it, every life is a pile of good things and bad things. The good things don't always soften the bad things, but vice versa – the bad things don't necessarily spoil the good things or make them unimportant. And we definitely added to his pile of good things.'

This fixed point might remain fixed but Amy's humanity and the Doctor's increasing sympathy for such emotion makes for a more uplifting cocktail than we have seen in previous series. Such deaths as van Gogh's are as inevitable as pain, as change. Time is the catalyst of change and in *Doctor Who* where time is bent in ways we cannot muster in real life, our regrets are challenged. *Doctor Who* is not about time travel because it does not rely on romanticising the past, or the future. It celebrates the present, what we have right now. It's telling you that even if there were other paths you could have taken, this is the one you are on. Do your best with it instead of wishing it away. I can never attend the funeral of my grandfather but if a TARDIS showed up on my doorstep and I was offered the chance to go, I don't know if I would. There's a beauty in the possible that *Doctor Who* recognises, posited against the dangers and sadness of the impossible. As individuals we will never be given the chance to change the past, for better or worse, and *Doctor Who* sees that as something to celebrate. The choices behind you are behind you and the only paths available are onwards, whether they be left or right or topsy or turvy.

Attempting to define the mundane comes up against a few hurdles such as understanding that no two people have the same life, the same experiences, so what is mundane to you might be a riveting thrill-ride to someone else (I hear not everyone loves *Doctor Who* and this is outrageous). Instead of considering mundanity as a result of subjectivity, I want to utilise it in the way I think the show intends – as a contrast to the impossible and the fanciful, as a presentation of what we are able to do with what we have and that being enough.

Interlude 1
and

'Just promise me one thing. Find someone.'
– Donna Noble.
Episode 14, Series 2
(The Runaway Bride)

Without their companion, there would probably be no Doctor. Or, at least, they would be flying through space without a human hot mess to keep them both grounded and, in all likeliness, motivated with annoyance. Since 1963, the Doctor has largely had someone by their side, with only a few notable exceptions. The episodes where the Doctor *does* travel without a companion tend to be *about* the Doctor's loneliness and how that makes them a little bit more alien. 'The Runaway Bride', the Christmas special that follows Rose's departure from the show in series two, specifically engages with this. In the climactic battle against the Racnoss, a deadly spider monster, Donna sees the Doctor's unforgiving side. In the burning lab beneath the river Thames, the Empress of the Racnoss watches her children drown as the Doctor stands motionless, allowing them to die. Somewhere between giving him permission to leave and begging him to see sense, Donna has to step in, saying, 'You can stop now.' When the Doctor asks Donna to come with him, she turns him down, horrified of the life he lives. She wants no part in it.

'You've seen it out there,' he tells her, trying to convince her to join him. 'It's beautiful.'

'And it's terrible,' Donna shoots back. 'That place was flooding and burning, and they were dying, and you stood there like... I don't know. A stranger.'

For all of the Tenth Doctor's humanity, it took one adventure without a full-time companion for his behaviour to devolve into drastically dangerous. Donna leaves him with some parting wisdom.

'Just... promise me one thing. Find someone.'

'I don't need anyone,' he claims. Donna sees right through him.

'Yes, you do. 'Cause, sometimes, I think you need someone to stop you.'

There's a visible realisation in his eyes that he's better

when he has someone next to him, someone to whom he isn't a stranger. As viewers, we know this instinctually. Humans by their very nature are reliant on other for biological, neurological, and psychological health, 'our bodies actually tend to work better when we're not alone. Being lonely has been linked to worse physical and emotional health outcomes and poorer wellbeing'.[1] Beyond the physical, a 2008 study that found judging a hill's incline was affected by the presence of friends – a hill was perceived to be less steep when the subject had a person of positive social support near them.[2] Those without friends near tended to exaggerate how steep the hill looked to be. Maybe if the Doctor stood solely at the base of a mountain, they'd be less likely to make a crucial trek than with a companion to give them the perspective and confidence they need to reach that summit.

The Doctor and companion Martha Jones, introduced in series 3's 'Smith and Jones', present a rebound-like dynamic after Rose's more romantically-coded relationship with her Doctor. Would the Doctor, facing that hill to climb, feel supported by Martha in the same way he had by Rose? Early on, the Doctor is struggling with Rose's absence, Martha seemingly unable to fill that gap. The Doctor takes Martha to places he visited with Rose ('Gridlock') or comments that 'Rose would know' the answer to their Shakespeare-themed threat ('The Shakespeare Code'). Grief is poisoning a potentially burgeoning relationship and this much is clear, at least to Martha, who harbours an unreciprocated crush on the Doctor.

However, by the two-parter episodes of 'Human Nature' and 'The Family of Blood', the Doctor puts his trust in Martha in a way he has done with no one else. When he must transform himself into John Smith, a vulnerable human without his alien abilities to keep himself safe, Martha is entrusted with his life. In the series' finale episodes, 'The Sound of Drums' and 'The Last of the Time Lords', the whole damn plan relies on Martha walking the entirety of planet Earth, for a year, alone, fulfilling the Doctor's instructions. She is entrusted with this as the Doctor is captured, kept prisoner, and she knows the responsibility that has fallen to her. This relationship is one-sided, with the Doctor asking a huge amount of Martha, and Martha giving willingly, out of love. She is pushing herself up the hill, but he is not helping her.

After the events of the finale, Martha walks away from the Doctor, permanently. She explains her motives through a relatable human experience from her past, a friend who also pined through unrequited love. 'He never looked at her twice. I always told her "get out". So, this is me. Getting out.' She saw the weight the Doctor put on her shoulders and while she was strong enough to carry it, she was also strong enough to know he should never have asked that of her, that this relationship was unbalanced and she was done with it.

Martha is hardly the only example of one-sided dynamics in *Doctor Who*, but she is a rarity in that she walked away of her own accord. Whittaker's Thirteenth Doctor describes this in 'The Haunting of Villa Diodati', that the relationship between the Doctor and their companions is never as simple as friendship, or romance. 'Sometimes this team structure isn't flat. It's mountainous, with me at the summit, in the stratosphere. Alone.' On the one hand this could be a kindness, taking the weight of tough decisions off the companions. On the other, it could be arrogance, but it's never malice – the Doctor doesn't intend on hurting the people they travel with. 'My friends have always been the best of me,' the Eleventh Doctor says. The Doctor needs his companions to keep him sane or grounded, even if he hurts them in the process. It might sound selfish, then, for the Doctor to do this but who amongst us doesn't need someone?

Through companions, *Doctor Who* also reminds us that they are not forever, The Doctor is just as fallible as the humans they travel with. Every relationship, romantic or platonic, familial or friendly, has its differences, its foibles. *Doctor Who* steps into the fray of complicated relationships, having characters figure out what they mean to each other, how they impact each other, for better or worse. And we must remember, the Doctor is not human. They do not age like we do, nor die like we do. They do not live a human life so why would we expect them to experience relationships in the same way? In a similar fashion to how the show makes fanciful sci-fi the antithesis of the beautiful human mundane, the Doctor-companion dynamic reveals something by contrast. For a relationship to work, what's needed is equal footing, respect and honesty. The Doctor is not equal, doesn't always respect, and constantly lies, even about something as simple as their name. No wonder they have a new companion every few years. This, however, demands of us an introspection – are we, in *our* relationships, equal? Respectful? Honest? If not, *Doctor Who* asks, how can you expect to maintain long-term, meaningful companionship?

Chapter 2
Relative

'*You're my daughter and we've only just got started. You're gonna be great. You're gonna be more than great. You're gonna be amazing, you hear me?*'
— **The Tenth Doctor.**
Series 4, Episode 6
(The Doctor's Daughter)

When the metaphorical hill can't be scaled with a companion, a friend, who else might we turn to? Family, biologic or chosen, is often the next go-to, if not the first. Pondering who I would want to scale such a hillside with, rather than thinking about who would be the perfect companion, I realised this theoretical ascent would be so much smoother with a group. As they say, it takes a village.

Forgive the morbidity of my anecdotes, but a moment of my life that comes to mind is the funeral of my great-aunt. This one I did attend, in 2017, travelling with my family from Cumbria to Dorset, spending a dour night with a family friend before heading to the service the next day, all packed like sardines in one car, listening intently to BBC Radio 6 Music as a way to distract from the day ahead. An emotional mountain, scaled in a tight metal box. Nana Barbara (as she was to the whole family, regardless of exact relations to her) was known for sharp humour that could look, to the uninitiated, like being a grumpy git. It felt fitting, then, that as we drove through a beautiful natural area towards the crematorium, the radio chose to play the theme to 1973 classic *The Exorcist*, 'Tubular Bells', with its universally-recognised, endless creepy piano riff. It was hilarious. We became delirious, cackling madly on our way up to the cremation, knowing wholeheartedly that had she been there, Nana Barbara would have been laughing just as loud. We later shared the story with the wider family, invariably met with gasps and chuckles, and a comment along the lines of 'she would have loved that.' That was the right group for that hill, able to share in the sadness and joy together, and climb to the summit.

Doctor Who's familial entanglements are, at times, a little less wholesome. We're talking timeline-demolishing pregnancy and estrangement in Amy, Rory and River, suffocating mother-daughter bonds in Jackie and Rose, tense adoptive relationships and tutor-student balance in Bill, and the Doctor's own familial connections, both biological (Jenny) and chosen (Wilf). Of all the companions and mothers and daughters and father-figures and Doctors in *NuWho*, it's impossible to pick out one connection more pertinent than another as they all exemplify a growth and perspective that can only be found in the presence of the counterpart. *Doctor Who* tackles familial relationships in ways only it can, looking at how these dynamics become messy, broken, and then fixed again. Far from mundane, maybe, but the show is mirroring our day-to-day existence whether we are happy with family or estranged or grieving. The core of the show always returns to the concept of family and why the everyday influence of family is to be celebrated, even in its darkest days.

Perhaps the most complex, intricate and high-concept family in *NuWho*'s run is Amy, Rory, River and the Doctor. It's been said 'if you've ever tried explaining to a child who River Song is and how her timeline works, you'll appreciate how overly complex the plots have become.'[1] So here I try to explain as though you are a five-year-old, why the Amy-Rory-River dynamic is well worth understanding for the pay off.

Throughout the first half of series six, Amy sees an odd woman appear in hallucination-like visions. In 'The Almost People', the Doctor discovers that Amy has actually been kidnapped whilst pregnant with Rory's baby, and the Amy that has been travelling with him all season is actually a decoy, a flesh-imitation with Amy's mind projected into it. All the while, the real Amy is slowly getting closer and closer to labour. She effectively wakes up nine months pregnant in 'A Good Man Goes to War', gives birth, and promptly has her baby, who she names Melody, stolen from her. A true-to-style bombshell moment reveals Melody Pond is actually River Song, the name being a mistranslation through history (or future, depending on how you look at it, if you're still following me!). Amy and Rory learn they can never save their daughter and bring her up as a child because River has already lived her life and knows that she wasn't raised by them. Amy's trauma from his tragedy follows her into the series seven when, in 'Asylum of the Daleks', she's been left unable to conceive. The chance to raise Melody/River leaves a hole in Amy and Rory's lives, one that can't be filled by another child of their own.

It seems unfair that Amy couldn't time/dimension-hop to that of adopted Bill Potts, the companion to Peter Capaldi's Twelfth Doctor, a member of staff at a university canteen with a foster mother named Moira. Maybe Amy could have been the mother to Bill where Bill struggles with the fostered relationships in her life.

When we meet Bill, she is hoping to learn by sneaking into lectures run by the Doctor, who is taking a break from TARDIS travelling after a tragic death. He does the unexpected and offers to become Bill's personal tutor. Despite Bill not being a student, the audience knows a companion offer when they see one. Trying to explain this to her foster mother, Bill says 'You know how you're my foster mum? He's like my foster tutor,' suggesting she sees the generous spirit in both figures in her life, new and old. Motherhood and tutorship, to her, are similar. However, as tutorship isn't an unconditional transaction where motherhood is much more likely to be (for better or worse), it puts a question mark over her relationship with Moira.

Comparatively, there's possibly no unconditional motherhood quite like Jackie's protective relationship over daughter Rose who are each other's rocks with no high-concept, time-jumping, identity-revealing, sci-fi tomfoolery. They live in a small flat in the working class coves of North London with their imperfect life as Rose is unemployed and out of education at nineteen years old. Their home suggests the plights of low-income, but there's a homeliness and warmth baked into every scene shared, with Jackie's unwavering loyalty and fierce protection of her daughter blazing out of the TV screen. It appears Rose also knows that whenever she needs, she can always go home to mum.

These variations of parenthood don't only extend to the companions, however. The Doctor has one of his most painfully human encounters in the face of his daughter, Jenny. The Doctor is repeatedly referenced to have been a parent with the most direct allusion to this in the aptly titled 'The Doctor's Daughter'. Through some science-y jiggery-pokery, a piece of the Doctor's DNA was extracted and extrapolated into human form. Jenny is his daughter – even her name, given by Donna, is a play on how she was 'generated' and not born. Of course, when the TARDIS unexpectedly throws him and current companions into Jenny's domain, being 'the only Time Lord' left, he's sceptical of Jenny's legitimacy, barely satisfied when a stethoscope reveals her two hearts, as only Time Lords have. 'You're an echo, that's all. A Time Lord is so much more. A sum of knowledge. A code. A shared history. A shared suffering. Only, it's gone now.' The Doctor doesn't just reject Jenny personally, but also culturally, denying her agency or even acknowledging the generational trauma that has surely made its way from his DNA to hers. She reflects everything he lost in his ultimate war, her hearts not equating to instantaneous father-daughter bonding. It's painful to watch Jenny yearn for answers, the Doctor only reluctantly offering up cryptic lines. But Jenny proves herself intelligent, charismatic, and much more like the Doctor than he ever expected, including the recklessness and self-sacrificial bits which we'll talk about later.

If conflict is the driver of storytelling, broken familial relationships must surely be the passenger screaming frantic directions. When viewed as a navigation of the distance between parent and estranged child, *Doctor Who* presents multiple arguably traumatic dynamics.

There's certainly much to be said about Amy and Melody/River's relationship as mother and daughter and the loss felt, Amy losing the ability to carry a child through a human timeline, Melody/River losing a childhood and parental figures she could have had. It's a difficult storyline to watch as it refuses to shy away from the all too human, all too complicated journey that is choosing to have a child or not have a child, if that is even an available choice, and choosing to be a present parent or not – or having that opportunity taken from you. We all envisage our lives to some extent, particularly where parenthood is concerned, and Amy, Rory and River represent a very nuanced and emotionally challenging path that comes with that vision, often mixed with hope and desperation in varying measures. Amy's pregnancy may have been supernaturally brief and River's life a long list of what-ifs, but *Doctor Who* gets to the heart(s) of what these relationships feel like for viewers beyond the script's page. It offers people who want to connect, who want family, an ultimately very human thing to seek.

Bill's search for familiarity is strained. There's a clear disconnect between her and foster mother Moira, partly evidenced by the fact that Bill hasn't disclosed her sexuality to her, apparent when Moira insinuates if she needs to be suspicious of the Doctor's intentions with Bill. Bill doesn't feel like anyone in her life has connected with her in a way that goes beyond that idea of 'fostering', she wants something more. The relationship between Moira and Bill is always shown layered with familiarity, comfort, and affection, the kind of I'm-sick-of-you that only comes with understanding that the person is going to be there at the end of the day. Unfortunately, Moira often *isn't* there at the end of each day and that's the issue. She is consistently distant, calling Bill to let her know she's not coming home or that she's coming back unexpectedly and interrupting a date. It's unpredictable and fleeting when Bill wants stability.

A conflict with Moira arises on Christmas morning (imagine a Christmas and no drama!) when Moira gifts Bill with money and says, 'I thought you'd enjoy choosing something for yourself as you're always passing judgements.' That same morning, Moira found a shoebox full of pictures of Bill's biological mum, something Bill has been desperate for. 'I didn't know we had them,' Moira says casually as she's getting ready to go out. To her, they're nothing. To Bill, everything. You can see a relationship strained on both sides, a comment quickly swept over in mutual exasperation. Loving the person who raised you without being able to like or understand them is a tragic skill many must learn to survive their upbringings and so, Bill looks elsewhere for the understanding she needs.

In one of the photos that she's now weeping over, she spots a reflection, an old man with a camera. The Doctor. At this point Bill doesn't know about the Doctor's origins, TARDIS, or time travel, all she sees is an impossible coincidence and possibly, the gift of understanding from her new tutor who somehow has a presence in her past and hopefully will do in her now-confusing present. Bill is depressingly comfortable with temporary figures. She tells us as much when she confesses to Moira that she doesn't learn Moira's boyfriend's names. 'I'll only get attached.'

The Doctor similarly struggles with connections that cannot last forever. 'You can spend the rest of your life with me, but I can't spend the rest of mine with you,' he says to Rose in series two, further exemplifying the power imbalance inherent to the Doctor's existence. If he is to be a foster tutor to Bill as she expects, at some point, his tutelage will end. The difference here is that Bill expects an end where Rose did not. Equally, the

Doctor isn't offering Bill a real place in the TARDIS because he knows, just like all the other companions, that he'll eventually have to say goodbye to her too. Their companionship is founded in pre-emptive grief, a reluctance to create a bond only to break it. Is this smart self-preservation or unnecessary self-inflicted isolation? How many of us have shut down as a means of avoiding pain? I expect every reader to raise their hand right about now, including Bill, if she was real, discovering something that audiences are more than familiar with – the various forms that family come in will not always be predictable nor even welcome, initially, if there is vulnerability at stake. As glib as it might be, it's true that the best things in life are often the most unexpected.

It's fair to say Jenny's appearance was an unexpected presence in the light of a somewhat mysterious Doctor. It's a subject not discussed in much detail across the show, but in the short snippets we do get, we see aspects of the Doctor's personality through themes of parenthood that aren't often presented in average episodes. The secret, vulnerable aspects come out to play in some of the most visceral ways.

'Donna, I've been a father before. I lost all that a long time ago. [...] When I look at her now, I can see them. The hole they left. All the pain that filled it. I just don't know if I can face that every day. When they died, that part of me died with them.'

No more detail is needed because the pain is plain to see. He is constantly moving on, always running, on to the next adventure. But framed in this way, around a family, his brief honesty becomes more significant. More than just in-universe lore, the Doctor's fatherhood suggests generational trauma from the war that destroyed his home planet of Gallifrey and everyone on it. A shared experience and culture lost, never to be understood by anyone else – unless they share his DNA. It's surely no coincidence that Jenny is a competent soldier, aware of the Doctor's similarities between his objective approaches to humanity and solid decision-making skills. While Jenny understandably steals the spotlight in 'The Doctor's Daughter', the fall-out of war is the main thrust of this episode, and how it ripples through generations, repeated time and time again, trauma shaping cultures, human bodies unable to truly forget. Only here, Jenny's not-so-human body also cannot forget, no matter how much the Doctor wants to deny it.

As the episode comes to a climax, two warring entities chase 'the Source', a weapon that is found to not be a weapon at all, but a terraforming device designed to bring life to the desolate world they're living on. But one man, a soldier, can't accept this outcome, needing to fight as it has been his life's purpose. The Doctor speaks of a brand new world full of life and potential and the soldier fires his gun. Jenny steps in between, taking the bullet to her chest, ultimately sacrificing herself. Dying in his arms, the Doctor pleads for Jenny to be strong. 'You're my daughter, and we've only just got started.' Falling quiet, he holds her, hoping that her two hearts will help her regenerate. Nothing happens.

Grief is a constant presence in *NuWho*, an unwelcome character in itself. In this episode we feel the Doctor's loss, aware that for a moment he had a true companion who could understand their origins and how that shapes their identities. But in this moment of loss for his species (again), we see something much more human than we have before. In Jenny, he initially faced reminders of a life lost, but in her death he has lost a daughter, a chance to forever hold a love that could span the regenerations that he could not spare for companions like Rose or Martha. I felt relief seeing the Doctor act this way. The acknowledgment that these emotions cannot be avoided, even by the most deft dodger of difficult emotions, validates the moments I've felt that loss, and have suffered from grief. It affords us recognition and company in those darker emotions, and tells us that grief is inevitable. It's how we cope that reflects who we are and our communities around us.

Of course, grief means that there was a bond strong enough to illicit a life-changing response and that only comes from a long-term, familiar relationship. 'Familiar' might be an understatement when it comes to Jackie and Rose. In 'Aliens of London', Rose and the Doctor return to Rose's home city for the first time since being whisked away, only to discover he's messed up the return trip. It turns out that Rose has been missing from London for a year, her mother, Jackie, beside herself with terror and now, understandably, rage. 'I've sat here, days and weeks all on my own! I thought you were dead! You waltz in here, all charm and smiles, and the next thing I know, she vanishes off the face of the Earth!'

After a justified smack to the Doctor's face, Jackie offers a teary-eyed plea to Rose for information on where the hell she's been for a year. A two-decade trust is being evoked, after a bond had been breached. 'What can be so bad that you can't tell me, sweetheart?' Until this point, there's likely not been much Rose hasn't told Jackie, but this? Time travel and flying police boxes? For Rose, it's impossible to explain. For Jackie, the fear of what happened in the twelve-month gap is heart-breaking. Every worst case scenario runs through her head. Of course, the truth does get out and does it affect Jackie's protective edge? Not likely.

A series later, in 'Love and Monsters', Jackie Tyler positively steals the spotlight. Events unfold from the perspective of Elton, a man who met the Doctor as a child and has chased him ever since. His sleuthing brings him to Jackie who he uses to get close to the Doctor. He fumbles when he forgets he has a photo of Rose in his jacket pocket, Jackie raging and demanding why he's searching for his daughter. Elton tries to placate her by saying he's not looking for her but it blows up in his face and Jackie has her hero moment. 'Let me tell you something about those who get left behind because it's hard. And that's what you become. Hard. But if there's one thing I've learnt, it's that I will never let her down. And I'll protect them both, until the end of my life.' Despite being left behind as her daughter travels across time and space, seeing things she would have never thought possible, Jackie puts jealousy aside to protect her child. We should all hope to have this person in our corner because there is no fighter across the cosmos of the *Doctor Who* universe quite like Jackie Tyler.

While the Doctor may not have a Jackie, he does have a Wilf. As companion Donna's grandad, Wilf has a removed but warm relationship with the Doctor until 'The End of Time – Part One', when they sit together in a café following mysterious happenings amongst Wilf's friends, the Doctor darkly reflective as he recounts the prophecy of his death, fearful that he could actually really, *really* die if he's injured before regeneration can take hold.

'Even if I change, it feels like dying,' the Doctor says in a morbid reflection of regeneration. 'Everything I am dies.' It's poignant and sombre, not the kind of conversation the Doctor could have with any of his other companions. In a later scene, Wilf shares his own fears, bringing out his old gun from the war. He tries to offer it to the Doctor but is refused. Wilf had the gun on himself when they were up against the Master, so the Doctor asks why he didn't use it.

'Too scared, I suppose,' Wilf says, the gentle soul that he is.

The Doctor looks at him, half a smile on his face. 'I'd be proud.'

'Of what?'

'If you were my dad.'

When you enter someone's life and have an impact, your potential future departure doesn't take away from all the meaningful moments once shared. In fact, there's beauty in the fleeting, in the temporary. The Doctor themselves is a constant, immortal being, yet is always in a state of flux, both as a single Doctor and following regeneration. One of the few things constant in the Doctor's life is family – it's just that the cast changes with time. Just as all humans are in flux with their own identities partly because of the people who come and go in our lives and their various influences/pressures, the Doctor is exactly the same – no more special, no more mundane – they just are and we just are.

When the Doctor leans on Wilf's father-like wisdom for just a moment, before the end, it's two old men sitting and talking, exchanging words of love and kindness in the face of certain doom. Wilf and the Doctor don't just talk, they deeply affect each other and recognise spectrums of joy and darkness not necessarily seen by others outside of the familial bond. This is the other side to the coin of Bill's relationship with the Doctor. Bill's tragically temporal experiences and relationships are unreliable and so life is unstable and she looks to the past for guidance where she finds a new temporary companion in the Doctor, but no less effective. In Wilf, we know that fleeting impacts are still impacts. The Doctor may has lived thousands of years and gathered knowledge far beyond human understanding but he is able to find solace in the company of an old veteran from London and despite only knowing his daughter for a splinter of time, she pushes his iron-clad objectivity to the limits, hopefully learning that he doesn't have to be completely alone in the universe, whether his companion shares his DNA or not. You can live a hundred lifetimes, but everybody needs someone in a moment, now and again.

I'd like to suggest you think on times you've disagreed with your family. Maybe over something small, maybe something life-altering. Maybe for no good reason, maybe for reasons all too important. Maybe it was something you were able to push past, maybe it was best for everyone involved to *not* to push past it. Whatever the reason and the outcome, do you ultimately feel that family has shaped you and continues to today? Are you thankful for it or resentful or somewhere in between? There is, of course, no right answer here, just feelings to be recognised as essential building blocks of human experience – the mundane and the spectacular.

Families, and the relationships within them, can feel catastrophic, or revolutionary, so big that they eclipse everything else. *Doctor Who*, for all its bigger-than-life settings and stories, squarely prioritises the *emotional* truth that we feel in these situations. It pulls at threads of mundane magnitude that stem from everyday life and blows them up on the screen, and even then, only really manages to scratch the surface of human complexity.

For *Doctor Who*, family isn't just a complicated bond, it's a potentially time-and-space-bending bond of catastrophic importance to those who are tasked with keeping the Earth, and the universe, intact. Every time familial bonds risk breaking our characters down, they are eventually, in fact, built up, better equipped than ever to keep the world spinning. What can possibly be mundane about that?

Chapter 3
Dimensions

> *'The Time Lord has such adventures,*
> *but he could never have a life like that.'*
> **– Joan Redfern.**
> **Episode 9, Series 3**
> **(The Family of Blood)**

In recent cinema output, alternate universes and timelines are becoming more and more prominent. From Marvel's *Loki* and *Doctor Strange in the Multiverse in Madness*, to the Oscar-winning and frankly phenomenal *Everything Everywhere All at Once*, today's audiences are inundated by stories about alternative dimensions. Dimensions are tricky to explain but the Doctor tries a few definitions for his own universe. 'It's like an alternative to our world, where everything's the same, but a little bit different.' ('Rise of the Cybermen') Some are useless. 'Imagine a great big soap bubble with one of those tiny little bubbles on the outside. [...] Well, it's nothing like that.' ('The Doctor's Wife') Most alternative dimensions are results of 'flux' points, the opposite of fixed points, where prior events are open to be changed, creating that ripple effect across time that has spawned so many creative sci-fi stories for decades and decades. *Doctor Who*'s exploratory action is nothing without the complexity of these flux points, when its characters are forced to go off-map and tackle other same-but-different manifestations of themselves that ask a range of questions from the mundane 'What if I hadn't taken that job?' to the interrogational 'What if I had been able to save my gran's life?'

As opposed to the fixed points we discussed earlier, which are used to show characters that their monkey-paw-like wishes for a different life are misguided, these alternate worlds are welcoming, open-armed and full of temptation. That gran-based question wasn't hypothetical, by the way. Rose's on-off boyfriend Mickey has to ask himself that very question when he finds himself in an alternative version of Earth with Rose and the Doctor.

Mickey's time in *Doctor Who* is often spent with him as the butt of the joke, with the Ninth and Tenth doctors calling him 'Mickey the idiot', whether affectionate or not. 'He's not invited,' the Time Lord says as he recruits Rose for the first time. When the Doctor is finally convinced to let Mickey on board the TARDIS, he's smarmy in his reluctance to accept, 'Okay then, I could do with a laugh.' Rose can barely contain her own derision, 'No, great. Why not?' Not exactly the warmest of welcomes.

In 'Rise of the Cybermen', the TARDIS accidentally (possibly because of Mickey) winds up breaking through a volatile Time Vortex and landing in an alternate version of London, a version where Rose's father is alive, unlike in 'her' London, as we discussed in an earlier chapter. The drama of this episode is propelled by the Doctor's attempts to convince Rose not to go looking for her father after learning the TARDIS needs twenty four hours to charge up before being able to travel back home, and, probably predictably, Rose throws caution to the wind against the Doctor's requests, as does Mickey.

'I've got things to see an' all,' Mickey says with a half-smile.

'Like what?!' the Doctor yells.

'Well, you don't know anything about me, do you? It's all about Rose. I'm just the spare part.' There is quiet glee underneath the sadness in what he says as he knows that the Doctor will chase Rose to the ends of the Earth, leaving Mickey to his own devices.

'Back here, twenty-four hours,' the Doctor orders as he predictably runs after Rose.

'Yeah,' Mickey says. 'If I haven't found something better.' And he does find better. Wracked with guilt over the death of his gran in his own dimension after he neglected to fix a loose patch of carpet on the stairs that caused her to fatally fall, he tracks down this parallel version of her and spots the same patch of carpet behind her in this new version of home.

'That carpet on the stairs, I told you to get it fixed. You're gonna… fall and break your neck.'

'Well, you get it fixed for me!'

'I should've done, way back. Guess I'm just kind of useless.'

Mickey's own self-flagellation and the Doctor/Rose's dismissal of his needs is a noxious cocktail, only rectified by leaving his original home and peers behind. In this universe, he can start again without starting again, a dream for many. When the parallel version of him dies, Mickey takes up the space and has a do-over, a chance to make amends and, crucially, celebrate a new-found self-confidence. This world presents Mickey with everything he's needed, everything Rose and the Doctor have denied him.

This is not the only time *NuWho* uses parallel dimensions to bring back the dead. In series eleven, Jodie Whittaker's Thirteenth Doctor meets her new companions Ryan, Graham and Yaz through a train crash. Later,

Ryan's grandmother Grace – Graham's wife – is tragically killed during an altercation with a malicious alien, Graham beside himself with grief as he holds her in her last moments. Ryan and Graham both struggle through the series to connect with each other as step-grandson and step-grandfather, having both lost the person who tied them together. Without Grace waiting for him at home on Earth, Graham is eager to keep travelling.

One adventure brings Graham painfully close to parallel temptations when in 'It Takes You Away', the Doctor, Graham and Yaz end up in a mirror world, a world flipped and warped and... perfect. Here, they meet a man whose wife died in the 'real' world, but somehow, in this dimension, she's alive and well. Happy, even. Urging him to stay, despite that he's left their blind daughter back in the 'real' world, Graham finds the same temptation waiting for him, backdropped by the stunning Norwegian landscapes and golden-hour sunbeams which make the scene almost heavenly. He finds Grace in the garden, by the clothesline, as alive as he's ever known her. 'Don't do this to me,' he says as they stare at one another, loss and love written on Graham's face.

'Am I real?' Grace asks. 'That creature [...], it killed me.' The sense of longing, of hoping this is real, is thick in the air, but just as potent is the knowledge that of course, it isn't. The first sign that things aren't as they seem comes when Graham expresses doubt and Grace shifts her intonation from being unsure as to whether she's *the* Grace to 'I'm here, love. I'm real.' This is a supernatural creature playing on Graham's vulnerability, drawing him in as it has done others in the episode. This maliciously conscious universe doesn't want to be alone, so it gathers human collectibles at their most vulnerable.

Emotional catharsis comes when the team discover that Ryan is caught in a terrible place between these two worlds and that they have to save him. Grace (or what is pretending to be Grace) tells Graham that he'll be fine, and the façade cracks. This charade is not Grace, the real Grace would never put her grandson in danger like that. Graham is pushed to realise the truth – that he needs to return to his real life, to reject the fantasy in front of him. Graham's choice is the core of this episode's story, becoming a beacon for anyone who has lived through an experience so horrible that avoidance feels like the only coping mechanism. Escaping reality is not a solution that benefits everyone and we have a responsibility to each other – we must work to process our pain and grief adequately so that we can take better care of others in their time of need, and of ourselves. Both Graham and Mickey's stories are driven by how grief can be handled when a second chance is seemingly dangled in front of you. Mickey is shown a better life, one that is real, that he's welcome to stay in with no other-worldly repercussions. It suggests it's possible to leave a comfortable but stifling situation behind to move on. Graham is shown a better life, but the life is a lie, an alien illusion. Graham is made to choose between this perfect fantasy and a reality of loss where he must make peace with what is gone and focus on what he still has. Reality cannot be ignored any more than grief can be fast-tracked. It will always come calling because, beyond whatever thin veil of fantasy we might weave for ourselves, our will problems wait for us.

To further wade through the misery of human experience, alternate dimensions don't just remind us what has been lost, but also what can never be gained. The series three two-parter 'Human Nature' and 'The Family of Blood' introduces a pocket watch. No ordinary pocket watch, this timepiece enables a Time Lord to shroud themselves by genetically re-coding their entire body into human form, with a lack of fantastical abilities and all. Using it to hide from the titular Family, the Doctor takes on the human identity of John Smith, a school teacher in 1913. John, like so many other humans, falls in love. It's the worst timing (after all, love isn't always on time) as in this realm, the Family are abducting, possessing and replacing locals to gather power, to the point that people are dying and the Doctor is necking with the nurse, Joan Redfern. The awkwardness of it is palpable and yet completely relatable. The world is scary, and impossible, ridiculous things happen every day, and yet people still find the time to fall in love. It can be frustrating to those who are watching from the outside, with Martha and the audience thinking *What are you doing? Aliens are coming! Keep it in your pants!* But it's easy to forgive connection when it's something so profound as the Doctor and Joan's. That is, until it endangers others.

John Smith is no Doctor we know, he flounders in the face of danger and carries all the prejudices of the early 1900s, dismissing Martha as she plays the maid role to blend into the environment. When the villains of this episode discover who John really is, they take both Martha and Joan at gunpoint, sneeringly throwing the Doctor's newfound connection back at him. 'Which one of them do you want us to kill? Maid or matron?' Tension doesn't come from the choice, the audience knows by now what has to happen. Instead, discomfort arises from knowing that the person making the decisions right now is experiencing something we've seen before in John – avoidance.

Because John is not real, he is without core memories and experiences as Joan finds out during an earlier conversation. Joan wants to know all about his past, about his upbringing in Nottingham, 'all those secret little places and dens and hideaways that only a child knows' but he can only list geographical facts like an encyclopaedia, which is effectively what John Smith is. Her heart is breaking because he doesn't have an answer and thinks he's hiding something monumental. For the audience, relief. For the two humans, Joan Redfern and John Smith, this is a moment of harrowing tragedy and loss of what has never truly been. *Doctor Who*, in one of its most bittersweet moments, gives the couple a glimpse into the life they will never have. John is desperate to live, positing that they could give the pocket watch to the Family. 'If they want the Doctor, they can have him!' But Joan reads the diary John has been keeping. 'I never read to the end. Those creatures would live forever. To breed and conquer. War, across the stars. For every child.' All at once, the setting of 1913 makes sense as we're now witnessing sacrifice known across generations. Joan has seen pain, war, death. She knows what it would mean to be selfish and her life with John is incompatible with peace. Not only must he die, he must give his life to another and another man will live in his place. As the fight rages around them, they curse the pocket watch and the tragedy it brings.

For all his calm and collected behaviour in the face of those who must die at Pompeii, for his steadfast belief that fixed points must be upheld, it's almost unnerving to see the Doctor so human, so aware of his emotions at a point of flux. We know that John Smith is not the Doctor, so this human vulnerability will not be carried on in the same way but we do wonder if this experience will bring more empathy to the Doctor's future actions.

He's all about saving swathes of people and planets and timelines, maybe this could inspire him to consider the sole human when necessary, when only raw emotion will get you through the upcoming hurdles.

But what of the more mundane choices we must make, ones that aren't fuelled by grief and lost love? What difference could choosing to take one job over enough possibly have on our lives and the wider existence of humanity? In *Doctor Who*, it turns out the stakes are high. 'Turn Left' presents companion Donna tricked into re-writing her own history after being sent back to a choice she faced before meeting the Doctor, taking a highfalutin city job or sticking with being a temp. She had, in the past, taken the left turn that lands her in London in 2006 with a fancy new job, leading her to the plot of 'The Runaway Bride'. She now turns right, staying in her temp job, far away from the Doctor's escapades and, crucially, she is not there to save his life. His death means there is no protector when every invasion and tragedy of series three and four take place until Britain is a dystopic hell-space where a nuclear-powered space-Titanic crashes into London, killing millions. What's left of the UK struggles to survive and we watch with Donna as the country slips into totalitarian nationalism. It's laughable that, in this context, Donna thinks of herself in a similar manner to the way

Mickey did, full of self-doubt and uncertainty. 'I'm nothing special.' This temp from Chiswick made one decision and brought down the entirety of the United Kingdom. Not even the most ardent Tory can manage that.

We are confronted with *Doctor Who's* mantra that is reaffirmed in John Smith's romance – there isn't a single ordinary person who isn't important. Even in the midst of an apocalyptic scenario, when the whole world is at stake, we are asked to focus on the importance of one person. The show celebrates how incredible ordinary people are, how the whole world could be different because of our throwaway choices. This attitude carries *Doctor Who*, like the charming line from Matt Smith's first Christmas Special, 'Nobody important? Blimey, that's amazing. Do you know, in nine hundred years of time and space, I've never met anyone who wasn't important before.'

And important we all are. Thanks to *Doctor Who*, we are reminded that while we are a tiny pin point in an infinite universe, we are important because we love and we lose, we grieve and we imagine another time where the other halves of our hearts are thriving, wishing we could join them. The real tragedy is the just-out-of-reach what-ifs that alternate dimensions offer. Though the Doctor has a life that many envy, he will never have the honour of a life filled with love and extraordinary normality. As Joan, his would-be wife says, 'The Time Lord has such adventures. But he could never have a life like that.'

It's a blessing, *Doctor Who* says, that we can live our lives at all.

Interlude 2
in

> 'You can spend the rest of your life with me,
> but I can't spend the rest of mine with you.'
> – The Tenth Doctor.
> Episode 3, Series 2
> (School Reunion)

The Doctor is an alien and at times, we must treat him as one. We've considered how the Doctor needs a human companion to counteract their objectivity and to ensure they don't completely lose whatever shred of humanity they might have in the face of an ongoing tragedy. However, the Doctor doesn't always truly *see* humanity, and all that comes with it, as something to be celebrated. The Doctor is just as likely to hold up a companion's humanity on a pedestal as they are to deride human naivety and simplicity.

In 'Bad Wolf', the Ninth Doctor tries to find Rose inside Game Station, a re-fitted version of TV station Satellite Five, only to discover someone has quietly hijacked the station and is using it to hide a signal beneath game-show broadcasts. Each broadcast is a throwback to a beloved British TV show, twisted versions of *Big Brother* and *The Weakest Link*, all with lasers and death sentences. A staff member begs the Doctor to let her and the staff go but makes the mistake of trying to shirk the responsibility of the lives taken by the corrupted telly shows. 'That's not fair. We're just doing our jobs.'

'With that sentence you've just lost the right to even talk to me, now *back off*!' Christopher Eccleston's Ninth Doctor isn't one to mess around. The staff member wants to argue that it's not her fault, the deaths of the contestants are far from her responsibility as she's not even involved in the shows themselves, but we can feel the poorly-veiled guilt under her pleading. The Doctor sees through it, making it clear he holds her at least partly responsible. Blindly following orders from above is not going to fly. This isn't to be mistaken as the Doctor looking down on humans or seeing them as lesser because of their profes-sional hierarchies (though you have to wonder what he thinks of unions). He's holding her, and her staff, to a higher standard. He motivates her to challenge orders. She later takes up arms alongside the Doctor in the episode's climax, inspired to do make amends.

We see a similar disappointment from the Eleventh Doctor when, in 'The Beast Below', he learns humanity has captured a Star Whale, the last of its kind. The Star Whale is big enough for an entire country to be strapped to its back and travel through space, but as they can't guarantee its cooperation, it is tortured and trapped to ensure the survival of the colony. In this circumstance, without the whale, all of Britain would be left adrift in space, to ultimately die, but the brutalisation of this creature cannot be ignored.

The Doctor is in a moral quandary. Freeing the whale will kill millions. Letting the whale die will mean he's directly responsible for the death of the last of its kind – just like he is. He finds a horrific middle-ground that would effectively lobotomise the creature so it wouldn't feel the pain of what humanity has done and continues to do to it. As people are desperately trying to think of something, *anything* that can be done to appease all parties, the Doctor is simply furious to have been put in this position.

This time, before the Doctor goes through with his plan, Amy makes the connection between the Doctor and the Star Whale and, without permission, pushes the button to free the whale. Instead of fleeing or attacking as expected, the Star Whale continues on its path as normal, seemingly unperturbed, revealing the subjugation wasn't needed. The Star Whale ultimately volunteered its help.

'If you were that old and that kind, and the very last of your kind... you couldn't just stand there and watch children cry,' Amy says. She'd seen that behaviour before, in the Doctor. His lack of emotional intelligence and ability to connect with the hypothetical in the way Amy can almost led to a horrible fate for an innocent creature, even if his intention was merciful. This push and pull between logic and emotion is constant.

In Capaldi's second episode, 'Into the Dalek', the Doctor is painfully clumsy when introducing his companion, Clara.

'This is Clara, she's, er, some other word.'

'I'm his carer,' Clara quips, a jab at his perceived age.

'Yeah, carer. She cares so I don't have to.'

That's certainly accurate of the dynamic the characters enjoy playing with early in this season, this new Doctor struggling to connect emotionally therefore leaning heavily into intellect and logic, letting Clara head-up the emotional, more human-oriented facets of their adventures.

A series later, 'Under The Lake' presents a Doctor completely thrilled by the idea of ghosts and it's up to Clara to sombrely remind him that for ghosts to exist, people have had to die. She pulls him away and shows him some flashcards made specially for him, a reminder of how to care for humans. They cycle through a couple, one of which says, 'I didn't mean to imply that I don't care.' Eventually he lands on the right one. 'I'm very sorry for your loss,' he says, sounding pretty earnest. 'I'll do all I can to solve the death of your friend, slash family member, slash pet.' A great joke, it highlights this particularly alien version of the Doctor and bridges the social gap between the species. The Twelfth Doctor struggles at this point in his life, a place where masking is essential for the purposes of blending in with humans. He simply doesn't understand what they care about or how they don't care about the phenomena *he* cares about. In this case, *ghosts!*

In 'Midnight', Tennant's Doctor accidentally reveals a previously hidden attitude. It's a pressure-cooker situation in this bottle episode that unfolds entirely inside a compact sci-fi bus. Passenger Skye is possessed and repeats her fellow passengers' words back at them, listening, learning. The Doctor deduces that the final stage of this apparent possession will be literally becoming the people that are parroted, and that becoming *him* would be particularly bad.

'Oh, like you're so special,' one of the passengers spits.

'As it happens, yes I am.' A quick and palpable anxiety is felt as the other passengers are insulted in the face of this arrogance. As events take a turn to the more threatening, the others begin to turn on the Doctor, convinced that throwing the possessed Skye out into the toxic atmosphere of the planet they're situated on would solve the problem. The Doctor, true to form, tries to take charge, to save Skye, but this time there's resistance. His charisma is not charming them as it usually does with other humans. The passengers pick up on the fact that he, in his usual excitement to meet a potentially new life form, is enjoying himself just a little bit too much.

'You've been loving it,' one accuses.

'You do seem to have a certain... glee,' another observes.

The tension builds, he's losing the crowd.

'You called us humans, like you're not one of us!' one shouts.

In this shameful moment of tribalism rooted in fear and aggression, it becomes clear what's happening. In the past, the Doctor's otherness has been a strength, offered a uniquely stance objective stance, but now it's weaponised against him. To them, he's not a Time Lord, not someone to be revered, he's just someone *different*. The situation devolves and characters dig their heels in until the Doctor snaps, asserting why he should be in charge, 'Because I'm clever!' They pause then scoff. To the Doctor, his intelligence means he should be in charge. Why wouldn't you trust and follow the smartest person in the room in a life or death situation? Unfortunately, he fails to recognise how his visible ego, no matter how accurate, alienates him from the group and once his ill-considered wording has insulted the last passenger, he's unable to take it back.

The Doctor is an alien, living amongst humans, travelling with them but no matter how much time he spends with us, fighting for us, he isn't human. That otherness manifests in loneliness, anger, and superiority, and is a characteristic the Doctor must learn to live with. Ironically, the Doctor's experience in being othered is incredibly... human. Through the Doctor, we see everyday moments of being unable to relate to your fellow man, mis-reading situations, or feeling like you're in a group that doesn't truly understand you. In more serious ways its systemic, built into racist societies and totalitarian governments, with millions and millions of people struggling through life at the hands of such othering. While the Doctor is attempting to improve the global, he has to feel the motivation of the local, of the human beings in front of him, before he can succeed in his missions.

Through the Doctor, we see ourselves and humanity in ways that are memorable and affecting. Just as the Doctor is unable to see himself in the Star Whale until Amy steps in, *Doctor Who* confronts human behaviour, especially when it's frightening or ugly. Both in how the Doctor perceives humans, and in how humans perceive the Doctor, opposing sides of otherness and group-think are evident. The Doctor's inhumanity becomes a way for us to explore what it means to be human, and to be part of your chosen in-crowd. But *Doctor Who* doesn't stop there. It offers us a hand, letting us forgive ourselves for falling short from time to time, so long as we try again and try better.

Chapter 4
Space

'At last, I know where I'm going, where I've always been going. Home, the long way round.'
— The Eleventh Doctor.
Season 7 , Special
(The Day of the Doctor)

Space is much like *Doctor Who* itself, finite yet endless all at once. There are about ten different definitions of 'space' in Merriam-Webster, though I will focus on two; 'the region beyond the earth's atmosphere or beyond the solar system' and 'physical space independent of what occupies it'.[1] Doctor Who flies through the first and humans are more used to navigating the second, where we have 'space' for movement, meeting, orienting. In *Doctor Who*, both versions of space are traversed to either save someone's home or to go home. It doesn't matter the setting, the location, or the people; there always seems to be a home at stake. Companions are repeatedly leaving their Doctors for home, eventually pining for their personal space, or the Doctor themself is lamenting Gallifrey and family, their version of what could have been home. No manner of space adventures can compare to the cosy, home comforts of a familiar roof over the head and a cup of tea in bed. Eventually, we always want to return to the mundane, to rest, to familiarity, even if we know we're going to leave, only to come back all over again. Even the Doctor can eventually appreciate and understand that so how can he make space a home?

There comes a time in most people's lives when they leave home for the first time. For me, like many, it was moving for university. I found my passions and my people, friends who I will hopefully have for the rest of my life, and I fell in love with a part of the UK I plan to stay in for the rest of my life. At eighteen years old, I thought, *Oh,* this *is the real world.* Almost immediately after leaving university years later, like many, I had a wake-up call. Working a dead-end job to pay rent, my friends were busy either struggling to get by or being far more successful than me with some moving away, thinning out my social circle almost overnight. It was a sobering experience. For very different reasons, I found myself realising, *Oh, this is the real world.*

Series thirteen special, 'The Power of the Doctor', has a familiar atmosphere as it's Jodie Whittaker's final voyage and regeneration approaches. Much like the end of my university life, no more fun and games. But first, newbie companion Dan almost dies at the hand of a Cyberman and decides this is the last straw, this is his final TARDIS trip.

'I get it,' the Doctor says, solemn but understanding. 'Life's important. Home's important.'

It is. Dan, faced with a near-death experience, chooses to go back to reality of his own accord. While he's relatively unusual in *NuWho* for doing this, it's not an unfamiliar impulse. Rose looked at the end of the world, faced with the Earth's destruction, calls home. Amy and Rory consider the adventures that could be had and wonder if work and wedding parties are more appealing right now. *Doctor Who* sweeps people away for a time on adventures that seem too big, too incredible to be real. The whole universe opens up and everything in space and time is suddenly possible. It's overwhelming to the human mind that only knows Earth and its immediately surrounding planets. Then, just like that, it's over, it's time to go home and put up your feet. The mundane almost always wins.

Dan isn't the only character to come crashing back to Earth this episode. 'The Power of the Doctor' reintroduces some companions from *Classic Who*, prior to the *NuWho* generation – Ace and Tegan – to its current audience. Ace appeared alongside Sylvester McCoy's Seventh Doctor, Tegan alongside the Fourth and Fifth – Tom Baker and Peter Davison respectively. Each has their own grievance with the Doctor, having left their relationships in the 'unfinished business' territory back in their day.

Tegan's departure was one of immediate regret when in 1984's 'Resurrection of the Daleks' Tegan pulls away from her Doctor, no longer enjoying the adventures. It isn't until the Doctor leaves that she realises her mistake, but it's too late, she's been left behind. Ace, on the other hand, was a victim of the show's cancellation. Her final on-screen appearance was in 1989's 'Survival', the final episode of the classic series. She walks with the Doctor, imagining all the amazing times they are yet to share. Excluding additional media like books, audio dramas and comics based on this series, this is how Ace is left, wanting more but never having the chance due to the cut-throat business of television. How many beloved fictional characters have we said goodbye to because of TV executive budgets and viewing figures? It doesn't bear thinking about. Ace and Tegan were both unable to conclude their journeys the way they wanted or deserved, left in the lurch with nothing but space between the lives that were designed for them, and the lives they would have chosen.

However, they eventually have their revival when the Doctor is re-introduced to them in the offices of UNIT, an international military organisation which operated under the auspices of the United Nations, originally under the name of the United Nations Intelligence Taskforce. She's awkward.

'How've you been?'

'Like you care!' Tegan snaps. It's understandable, Tegan has felt abandoned by the Doctor, annoyed that they never came back to check in on her. When the Doctor is caught in the UNIT stronghold, Cybermen closing in, Tegan is curt again. 'I have spent the past thirty years living like a nomad. I have done landmines, coups, I have been hijacked and I've nearly drowned trying to help people. I've seen off two husbands, and somewhere out there is an adopted son who hasn't called me for six weeks.' Thanks to this bit of rapid exposition, the audience understands her frustration but also sees something else, a life filled with remarkably human experiences. Tragic, yes, but human all the same. Marriage, divorce, adoption, service, *these* are the adventures that can be waiting back home without the Doctor's intervention. These are the pockets in space that actually matter to the companions, eventually. Much like myself, going off to university, thinking it was the beginning of fun forever only to face reality a few years later, Tegan found herself back on Earth, but she had to make do with the tools the Doctor had left her with to make her new life her own which, as it turns out, ended up being far from mundane.

Dan's goodbye speech sums up this impulse in a nutshell.

'My life's far from perfect, but I need to get back to it. I need to attack it. I can now, because I've been with you.'

While Dan walks away of his own accord, Tegan regrets her choice. They represent two paths; one is a revelatory decision, another is thrust upon its subject without warning. The latter is usually when we then have to grapple with grief of what was lost and fear of what's ahead. Sometimes you don't get to choose whether to turn left or right.

Ace has a similar experience to Dan when she is met with a hologram-version of the Seventh Doctor, *her* Doctor. She is granted both reunion and closure in this one moment. The Doctor tells her, 'I was only ever trying to teach you good habits, Ace. Obviously I failed.'

'You never failed me, Professor,' Ace says. 'You made me the person I am today.'

It's a calm, charming moment that has a lot of unseen history on its shoulders, two fond friends separated by circumstance, reunited and given the chance to share who they've become. 'All children leave home, sooner or later,' the Doctor tells her. 'The joy is to watch them fly.' As I was watching this, I couldn't help but feel like Sylvester McCoy had been brought in to comfort me, specifically, offering the classic adage that the whole point of adventure is the lessons learned on the journey, it's not about the destination, whether it's space or home. Whatever the outcome, whether bruised and battered or not, being able to ultimately move forwards is a victorious destination to find yourself in. In *Doctor Who*, the Doctor is not home. The Doctors are not where the companions belong, not *really*. Home is always calling for them. The lucky ones get to go back.

For the Doctor, there is a very physical place they call home. Not Gallifrey, the Doctor's planet of origin, which is less of a home and more of a looming, haunting memory of ages past. Their home is inarguably the TARDIS. A chosen home as a vehicle, living space, and laboratory all at once, its rooms shifting to the Doctor's needs, infinitely big yet never unfriendly or unwelcoming. The TARDIS is an icon of all of *Doctor Who*. Even as the Doctor changes their face and companions come and go, the blue box is a staple. While the inside also changes, having had multiple looks across the *NuWho* era, there are always visually recognisable touchstones. The central column and console, the hexagon-shapes on the walls. They shift and change, but never leave. It's like the office from *The Office*, the flat from *Friends*, the sleeping quarters in *Red Dwarf*. The TARDIS is where the audience can feel safe, no matter how drastic the change around or within it.

Each incarnation of the Doctor can be interpreted by their console rooms. For the Ninth and Tenth Doctors, it looked a little ramshackle. Driving the TARDIS was often very tactile with lots of physical movement required to wrangle it like a bucking bull, sparks flying, a hammer on-hand to smack the console into submission if needed. There wasn't much room for furniture other than some cheap, torn-up chairs an appropriate distance away from the danger area, giving plenty of space to bound around. It was also dark and gloomy at times, needing the energy of the people within it for it to come alive. It reflected the torment and anger of the Ninth doctor, and the energy and exuberance of the Tenth.

The Eleventh Doctor featured a more fairy tale feel and so his TARDIS was larger, shinier, more inviting. There were several levels, which meant conversations could be shouted across the space, and characters could see through the glass floor, beneath the console where the Doctor worked. It was social. This TARDIS expected a larger group, welcoming people with glitter and fancy. This hinted at the Eleventh Doctor's tendency to collect people, his big group of 'strays'.

His second TARDIS was colder, the loss of Amy and Rory meant he'd looked for a machine that was just that, a machine. It was much more angular and metallic, with sharper edges replacing the previous sweeping scale. With the Twelfth Doctor, however, that TARDIS became a little softer, a little more lived-in. On the second floor there were bookshelves and chalkboards, places to investigate and think. This Doctor was no-nonsense, without time or patience for frills and fairy tales. He and the TARDIS were both more collected and methodical, but never without some warmth. His character was sometimes more logical than emotional, his space mirroring that clearly.

The Thirteenth's TARDIS is perhaps the darkest, the walls black and the floors grey, the space illuminated only by bright columns of glowing crystal. There is a clear mismatch between the dark mechanics and bright natural materials as the Thirteenth Doctor's sunny disposition and bubbling anxiety battle for dominance. There are columns of light within her, yes, but they are spotlights in a room polluted with darkness and mystery that even she doesn't know about.

Whether we realise it or not, our homes say a lot about who we are but the people within it say more.

The TARDIS's various outfits over the years show how a home is shaped by the person living in it and how they engage with that space. We think we build our spaces but our spaces react to us and can even betray us. Seeing how the TARDIS alters itself to fit the Doctor inhabiting it, I think about the different living rooms I have seen in my life. In student halls, the shared living space had more chairs than people, no personal touches, and a teetering pile of cans and glasses that grew in the corner window every weekend. My grandfather's was dressed with hard leather and deep brown furnishings that complimented his remarkable mix of warmth and briskness. My first flat, with books piled to the rafters due to a lack of shelves and cheap furniture, meant I could actually have friends round for movie nights. My friends' first house with Lego *Star Wars* figurines on the shelves next to the beautiful art piece over the fireplace, the mix of colour and fun they want to show off in their life.

The TARDIS has become *Doctor Who*'s fandom's adopted living room. When it's on the screen, we know that's where the Doctor and their companions will scheme, full of excitement like they're planning a holiday, where they have quiet, pensive moments that reflect the danger of the day. For us, home is where we retreat to at the end of a long day, just as many of us might do to a sofa with a cup of tea. For many, it means family and warmth, familiarity, rest and, ultimately, safety.

When not physically in the space of their homes, they can become baggage for the companions. Rose's bedroom is pink-walled and purple-floored, the walls wear pictures of people we will never see, and the bedside table is buried under masses of little tchotchkes. Her life is full, lived-in, and messy. It immediately puts us in the mind-space of a teenager who's struggling to make sense of it all.

Martha Jones is introduced, instead, on her way to work, navigating family phone calls, and we see snippets of *other* people's homes, busy and chaotic. The people around Martha are a mess, but *she's* getting on with it, cooler heads prevailing. It's not until later that we see Martha's home, a small student flat with a stereo system perched on a shelving unit, half-blocked by a clothes hamper. When we get a better look, we see pictures on the mantle, a sofa and working space. It feels like a temporary place, lacking attachment. As mundane as it gets.

Donna Noble is quite the opposite, an adult living at home with three generations under one roof. 'Home' isn't a place that belongs to her, it's an environment where she is treated as a child despite being the oldest companion to date, contrasted against two generations above her. This insight into Donna's abode was aired in 2008, during the global financial crash, and the struggles Donna faces at the time are all-too-accurate to the environment around her. Even now, Donna's situation represents what many people might be facing during rolling economic crises, the difficulty of affording a space of one's own and the struggle to hold down a job. Never mind worrying about whether that job might cause the apocalypse or not.

The companions carry these settings with them everywhere they go with the Doctor. It's where personality traits are established, flaws presented, and motivations calculated which ultimately lead them to the Doctor and their offer of space-time galivanting. Just like the different forms of the TARDIS, the homes and comfort spaces of each companion are manifestations of their characters. They give us, the audience, a shorthand into their state of mind, their lifestyle, and skip over the unnecessary waffle of exposition, while exemplifying the significance of the spaces we inhabit, as we likely sit in our own homes, watching on. Homesteads and the baggage they carry influence our outlook on the world, giving us context on how the companions change throughout their journey, and how their attitude to home changes.

Some are comfortable and could do with a change in their lives. Some are frustrated at being looked down on, not fulfilling what they feel is their real potential. Some are simply without attachment, lacking in any real reason to stay with *every* reason to go. Each space is their own, ever-evolving, its significance shifting and changing as much as any character.

If our homes can betray us, can we betray our homes? *Doctor Who* can, of course, and in 'The Doctor's Wife' the unthinkable occurs, the TARDIS is transformed into a person. Its soul is transferred into a human form, Idris, so that the villain, a consciousness known as House, can devour the TARDIS. When the Doctor lets slip that he's the last Time Lord, House steals the more useful time-travelling TARDIS, leaving Idris with the Doctor. While Idris runs around with the Doctor, she's able to talk to him.

'I was already a museum piece when you were young. And the first time you touched my console you said–'

'I said you were the most beautiful thing I had ever known.'

'Then you stole me. And I stole you.'

Their relationship is ancient and their history more intertwined and intimate than anyone else the Doctor has ever known. They have been together since before the Time War, or the death of all other Time Lords, through regenerations and companions. As the Doctor comes to terms with what – *who* – she is, he asks the questions he's never been able to before, like a name.

'700 years, finally he asks.'

There's flirting and arguing and collaborating, the

Doctor's excitement is undeniable. Their relationship is, admittedly, hard to define. The TARDIS is more than a vehicle, it's a character – and actual real, living and breathing character. This episode is surely a love-letter to the TARDIS who has been the other main character of *Doctor Who* since day one, bridging the Classic and *NuWho* series in ways no cast member or showrunner ever could.

'Hello,' Idris says in her final moments, before the body breaks up and she goes back to being the voiceless blue box we know and love. 'Hello, Doctor. It's so very, very nice to meet you.'

Her goodbye is our coming home after a long day, exhausted and burnt out, waiting to be hugged by a patient sofa. Silent and comforting, a home can be a best friend. So many life events happen in the home and are celebrated on its surfaces, photos on nightstands, baby-proofed stairwell, sofa legs chewed up by the cat. We write ourselves all over the spaces in which we live, without ever expecting to hear anything back. *Doctor Who* gave the home a voice, and all it wanted to say was *hello*. How lovely it would be to know the spaces we call home felt just as fondly of us.

Conclusion
The Future

> 'You know, in nine hundred years of time
> and space, I've never met someone
> who wasn't important before.'
> — **The Eleventh Doctor.**
> **Episode 14, Series 5**
> **(A Christmas Carol)**

At the time of writing, the future of *Doctor Who* is at a turning point.

Jodie Whittaker's Thirteenth Doctor has just regenerated into David Tennant, which is *wild*. We know, within a handful of specials, Ncuti Gatwa will be taking up the helm. As it stands, the future is looking a lot like the past; David Tennant and Catherine Tate are back, as is writer Russell T. Davies. This is the team that brought in *Doctor Who*'s highest ratings ever so who better to usher in this new era? For the optimistic, it is a victory lap. For the doubters, it's a reassurance.

Everything is the same.

Everything has changed.

Children who, until now, have only seen themselves in companion roles or as side-characters, will now see someone who looks like them as The Doctor. They will see themselves out in the universe, doing the impossible, saving humanity from monsters and laughing all the way, navigating relationships, making mistakes, loving and losing. As someone who has seen themselves in the Doctor for over a decade, I am *so* excited to see how the show will find them, how it will inspire and move them the same way it did me. I'm excited to see, seventeen years from now, how the show will continue to grow and evolve, but I'm also excited to see how it continues to, as I interpret, celebrate the mundane. This conclusion is called 'The Future' and to look forwards, we must look back.

Eccleston's Ninth Doctor's departure shared a proclamation of achievement and self-forgiveness. 'You were amazing. And you know what? So was I!' Tennant's Tenth a yearning goodbye, a last wish for more time that isn't to be. 'I don't want to go.' In retrospect, this is all the more prescient given both the showrunner who penned them and the actors who embodied them are to return, albeit briefly. At his end, Smith's Eleventh Doctor is full of sheer joy for having lived his life, acknowledging that it was time to move on. 'I will always remember when the Doctor was me.' Capaldi's Twelfth's send-off was also that of showrunner Steven Moffat, his words thinly veiled in the Doctor's own, 'Doctor, I let you go.' The most recent words of Whittaker's Thirteenth Doctor, 'That's the only sad thing. I wanna know what happens next. Right then, Doctor whoever-I'm-about-to-be... tag. You're it.' While many of these speeches look back on themselves, she looks forward with an excitement for history to become now, for the world to go on in her wake, granting the propulsion needed to send the show into its next phase of life.

'Everything has its time and everything dies,' the Ninth Doctor says in 'The End of the World'. From the jump, *Doctor Who* has been aware of its own mortality and that of its subjects, the basis of human experience. This shouldn't be interpreted as nihilistic, but as inspirational and motivational as it's intended to be. The Eleventh Doctor later says,

> 'There is so much, *so much* to see, Amy. Because it goes so fast. I'm not running away from things, I'm running to them, before it flares and fades forever.'

My family moved from Dorset to Cumbria when I was eight years old. In a single day I left my school, my friends, and everything I was familiar with behind to move hundreds of miles across the country. The change was terrifying. Two years later, *Doctor Who* reassured me that change was part of life, important. I wish I didn't have to wait those two years before truly understanding that, as much as a ten-year-old can. Even if it was a surface-level understanding, any child going through a life change could benefit from having a fictional role model, especially a time-travelling one, to tell them point-blank: *change is okay*.

Reiterating the problem with this book's subtitle, *Doctor Who* isn't a show that celebrates mundanity, it's a show that insists no one should be seen as *mundane*, whether it looks to be from the outside or feels to be on in the inside. Characters from all walks of life are written to be extraordinary *because* of, and not in spite of, their apparent mundanity.

A nineteen-year-old with an under-paid job and strangled ambition. A single mum in a council flat trying to make ends meet. A temp from Chiswick who still lives in their mum's house. A trainee doctor from a broken home. A girl with an imaginary friend so real she went to therapy. A boy in love with his best friend. A daughter meeting her parents for the first time as an adult. A nanny-turned-teacher trying to make love work. A dinner lady who wants more than anything to learn. A step-family struggling to connect. A police officer trying to live up to family expectations. A man with empty cupboards. These people are not just companions of the Doctor, they are the mundane lives of extraordinary people. Each of these people, given the opportunity to go on incredible adventures, was allowed to show the incredible person they always were inside. The Doctor does not create interesting characters out of mundane ones, he finds people who are already amazing.

They are not just characters in a sci-fi show, they are the very real facets of our world. I know a lot of these people, and have myself been a few of them. They are full of potential and change, of histories and futures. They are me, they are you, they are people we know and see every day. This is how *Doctor Who* celebrates us – by showing off how amazing we are, already. *Doctor Who* presents *people*, flaws and all, and asks if we see ourselves in them. Then, it shows how extraordinary those people really were all along, daring us to acknowledge that, if these people can be extraordinary, then maybe we can too.

References

Interlude 1: and

1. "In good company: Why we need other people to be happy". Sarah DiGiulio, *Better*, 9 January 2018. nbcnews.com/better/health/good-company-why-we-need-other-people-be-happy-ncna836106. Accessed 26 March 2023.
2. "Social Support and the Perception of Geographical Slant" Schnall, Simone; Harber, Kent D.; Stefanucci, Jeanine K.; Proffitt, Dennis R., *Journal of Experimental Social Psychology*, 2008, doi.org/10.1016/j.jesp.2008.04.011. Accessed 3 December 2022.

Chapter 2: Relative

1. "Doctor Who: Steven Moffat's highs, lows and time-travelling hijinks." Martin Belam, *The Guardian*, 30 June 2017. theguardian.com/tv-and-radio/2017/jun/30/doctor-who-steven-moffats-highs-lows-and-time-travelling-hijinks. Accessed 26 March 2023.

Chapter 4: Space

1. "space". *Merriam-Webster*. merriam-webster.com/dictionary/space. Accessed 26 March 2023.

Acknowledgements

Firstly, thank you to Heather and Laura, for taking a chance on this. 404 Ink delivers incredible pieces, and it's a genuinely humbling honour to be given the chance to contribute.

Lucy, I don't think anyone would be surprised to hear that you are both my greatest critic and my deepest inspiration. Thank you for the shared long nights of coffee-induced madness, all those hours spent reading and giving me notes, and for watching hundreds of hours of *Doctor Who*. None of this could have happened without you.

To all those who have helped me by gracing me with their eyes and thoughts on my work, thank you. I won't list you all, because we'll be here all day, but you know who you are.

To my parents, who sat me down in front of the TV in 2005 to sit and watch 'Rose', I'm not sure you know exactly what beast you unleashed that day, but look at me now! Whodduthunk.

And, only because it would feel silly not to say, thank you to everyone who has ever been involved in making *Doctor Who*, in any and all of its forms. I'm sure I won't be the first nor last to tell you that this is a show that has changed lives and broadened horizons, and for good reason.

About the Author

J. David Reed is a working-class science-fiction and fantasy writer based in North-East England. He has had multiple short fiction pieces published, his most recent in dark fantasy anthology series *Dark Magic*. He is a qualified teacher and works for a charity that supports NHS workers with CPD, and is a lifelong fan of *Doctor Who*.

About the Inklings series

This book is part of 404 Ink's Inkling series which presents big ideas in pocket-sized books.

They are all available at 404ink.com/shop.

If you enjoyed this book, you may also enjoy these titles in the series:

Love That Journey For Me – Emily Garside

Considering the fusion of existing sitcom traditions, references and tropes, this Inkling analyses the nuance of *Schitt's Creek* and its surrounding cultural and societal impact as a queer revolution.

The Loki Variations
– Karl Johnson

By exploring contemporary variations of Loki, from Norse god to anti-hero trickster, we can better understand the power of myth, queer theory, fandom, ritual, pop culture itself and more.

Now Go
– Karl Thomas Smith

Now Go enters the emotional waters to interrogate not only how Studio Ghibli navigates grief, but how that informs our own understanding of its manifold faces.